be true

Sheri Martin

BALBOA.PRESS
A DIVISION OF HAY HOUSE

Balboa Press books may be ordered through
booksellers or by contacting:

Balboa Press
A Division of Hay House
1663 Liberty Drive
Bloomington, IN 47403
www.balboapress.com
1 (877) 407-4847

Print information available on the last page.

ISBN: 978-1-9822-4061-5 (sc)
ISBN: 978-1-9822-4060-8 (e)

Library of Congress Control Number: 2019921171

Balboa Press rev. date: 01/11/2020

this book has been created to encourage and inspire the journey of living true

each page has one thought to ponder contemplate and consider

the words are meant to offer an opportunity for personal reflection

the intention behind these writings is to encourage living a conscientious life a life that is based in kindness compassion and love

to my wonderful grandchildren Ava Bella Riley and Wyatt may you always do what you love and follow your dreams

be honest
and true
in all you do

awake
each new day
with
gratitude and wonder

imagine
living a life
that is
genuinely true

know
the value
of
our time here together

face
each and every
life challenge
with courage

reflect
on moments
that inspire
encourage and lift

be open to new
adventures
and unknown possibilities

embrace
loves presence
ever mindful of your choices

notice
the miracles
surrounding you
in each day

see
and truly appreciate
the
beauty of nature

set aside time
for yourself
to go play

strive
to make each day
a good experience

consider compassion
before using judgement
towards
one another

reach for a higher
state of
conscious awareness

look beyond
that which
is on the surface

get
outdoors and explore
and
connect with nature

seek
to explore lifes
abundance of
great mysteries

enjoy
music movement dance
and
basic physical activity

participate
in activity that
enhances
body mind and spirit

be
aware and gracious
of those
around you

recognize
when negative thoughts occur
and
release them

discern
what is of benefit
and
whats not

align
with the flow
of natures
divine energy

practice
new methods of thinking
in positive ways

patience
and
persistence
as you make personal
improvements

pursue
the desires
of your divine
spiritual nature

be
creative in expressing
your inner
divine self

embrace
opportunities to have fun
and
celebrate life

discover
personal solutions
to transform
negative to positive
within
each day

set aside time for
meditation

respect
the
great mystery of lifes
divine essence

be
actively involved
in that which
brings joy

center
your spiritual
physical
mental self in love

learn
to become aware
of
your personal thoughts

prepare
and take in
nourishing
types of food

determine
to release all
negative influences
and thoughts

let go
of
any and all
negative energy

honor
loves presence by
choosing to respond
kindly

look
towards desires
that fulfill heart
and soul

become aware
of
loves presence in
all things

consider
desired outcome when
making choices
in life

enjoy
the experience of
your
personal self expression

be mindful
of
your thoughts
throughout the day

discover
personal gifts and talents
and
develop them

offer
kindness
at every single
opportunity each day

move
with an attentive
mindset and heart

know
the beauty of
loves
divine universal existence

make time
to have
moments
of quiet stillness

generate
momentum
towards that which is
truly good

practice patience
and
compassion
when dealing with others

create time
for
searching the
depths of soul

create
an environment
of
encouragement care and love

share yourself
openly and honestly
when you
communicate

observe
and ponder
your personal
patterns of thoughts

engage
in conversation
when the opportunity
presents itself

learn to listen
to
your
inner divine wisdom

respect
the reality of
divine
instinct and intuition

ponder
contemplate and question
all things
in life

hold true
to that which
is good

always
keep
a written record
of your
lifes journey

discover
the experience of
keeping
a personal journal

be
honest and true
in all
you do

journal pages